EMMANUEL JOSEPH

Valley Vanguards and Realty Royals, Comparative Business Mastery

Copyright © 2025 by Emmanuel Joseph

All rights reserved. No part of this publication may be reproduced, stored or transmitted in any form or by any means, electronic, mechanical, photocopying, recording, scanning, or otherwise without written permission from the publisher. It is illegal to copy this book, post it to a website, or distribute it by any other means without permission.

First edition

*This book was professionally typeset on Reedsy.
Find out more at reedsy.com*

Contents

1	Chapter 1: The Dawn of Innovation	1
2	Chapter 2: The Foundation of Stability	3
3	Chapter 3: Risk and Reward	5
4	Chapter 4: Culture and Leadership	7
5	Chapter 5: Market Dynamics	9
6	Chapter 6: Funding and Capital	11
7	Chapter 7: Technological Integration	13
8	Chapter 8: Customer-Centric Approaches	15
9	Chapter 10: Global Expansion	19
10	Chapter 11: Sustainability and Ethics	21
11	Chapter 12: Future Trends and Challenges	23

1

Chapter 1: The Dawn of Innovation

In the heart of Silicon Valley, innovation reigns supreme. Pioneers like Apple and Google emerged from modest beginnings, driven by visionary leaders with a thirst for groundbreaking technology. Their success stories highlight the importance of embracing risk, fostering a culture of creativity, and leveraging the power of networking. By understanding the mechanisms behind their meteoric rise, we gain insight into the core principles that fuel tech-driven businesses. The entrepreneurial spirit in the Valley is not just about having the next big idea but about nurturing an environment where innovation can thrive. Each breakthrough, from the personal computer to the smartphone, showcases the transformative power of relentless pursuit and visionary thinking.

The culture of Silicon Valley is unique in its embrace of failure as a stepping stone to success. Companies often pivot multiple times before finding their winning formula. This resilience is embedded in the Valley's DNA, where the mantra "fail fast, fail often" drives continuous iteration and improvement. Startups attract top talent from around the world, creating a melting pot of ideas and perspectives. The collaboration between universities, research institutions, and industry players further fuels the cycle of innovation. The spirit of open-source development and knowledge sharing accelerates technological advancements, making Silicon Valley the epicenter of the tech revolution.

Leadership in Silicon Valley is characterized by bold visionaries who are not afraid to challenge the status quo. Figures like Steve Jobs and Elon Musk exemplify the power of charismatic leadership combined with unwavering belief in their mission. These leaders inspire their teams to push boundaries, think outside the box, and strive for excellence. The Valley's ecosystem supports a flat organizational structure, where employees are encouraged to take ownership of their projects and contribute to decision-making processes. This empowerment leads to high levels of motivation and creativity, driving the continuous cycle of innovation.

Funding plays a critical role in the success of Silicon Valley companies. Venture capital firms, angel investors, and accelerators provide the financial backing needed to turn ideas into reality. The availability of capital enables startups to experiment, iterate, and scale rapidly. The concept of "smart money" goes beyond just providing funds; investors offer mentorship, strategic guidance, and valuable industry connections. This symbiotic relationship between entrepreneurs and investors fosters an environment where risk-taking is encouraged, and groundbreaking ideas are brought to life.

In summary, Silicon Valley's success is built on a foundation of innovation, resilience, visionary leadership, collaborative culture, and strategic funding. This unique combination of factors creates an environment where groundbreaking ideas flourish, and technological advancements continue to shape the future. As we explore the stories of these Valley Vanguards, we gain valuable insights into the principles that drive their success and the lessons that can be applied across industries.

2

Chapter 2: The Foundation of Stability

Realty Royals, on the other hand, build their empires on the bedrock of stability. In the realm of real estate, the focus is on tangible assets and long-term value creation. The journey from land acquisition to property development requires strategic foresight, meticulous planning, and an in-depth understanding of market dynamics. The real estate moguls' ability to transform urban landscapes and generate consistent returns showcases a different breed of entrepreneurial skill. Their expertise lies in navigating regulatory frameworks, anticipating market trends, and constructing buildings that stand the test of time. Each project, from residential complexes to commercial hubs, reflects the careful orchestration of resources and vision.

The real estate industry operates within a framework of stability and predictability. Market trends are influenced by factors such as economic cycles, interest rates, and demographic shifts. Real estate moguls excel at analyzing these trends and making informed decisions that maximize returns. Their success is built on a deep understanding of the market and the ability to identify opportunities for growth. The emphasis on long-term value creation means that real estate investments are carefully planned and executed, with a focus on sustainable development and community impact.

Leadership in the real estate sector is characterized by experience, relationships, and a pragmatic approach to decision-making. Real estate moguls have honed their skills through years of industry experience, developing a keen eye for opportunities and risks. They build strong networks of relationships with stakeholders, from contractors and architects to government officials and investors. These relationships are essential for navigating the complexities of property development and ensuring successful project execution. The ability to balance short-term gains with long-term vision is a hallmark of effective real estate leadership.

Funding in the real estate sector typically involves a combination of equity, debt, and private investments. Real estate moguls leverage their assets to secure financing, often structuring deals to maximize returns while minimizing risk. Institutional investors, such as pension funds and real estate investment trusts (REITs), play a significant role in providing capital for large-scale projects. The ability to structure financing deals effectively is a critical skill for real estate leaders, allowing them to bring ambitious projects to life and achieve sustainable growth.

In summary, the success of Realty Royals is built on a foundation of stability, market understanding, experienced leadership, strong relationships, and effective financing. Their ability to transform urban landscapes and generate long-term value showcases a different breed of entrepreneurial mastery. As we delve into the stories of these real estate moguls, we gain insights into the principles that drive their success and the lessons that can be applied across industries.

3

Chapter 3: Risk and Reward

Both Valley Vanguards and Realty Royals are no strangers to risk. In Silicon Valley, the stakes are high, and the potential for exponential returns is ever-present. Tech startups operate in an environment where innovation and agility are paramount. This chapter examines how tech entrepreneurs manage risk through diversification, pivoting, and continuous learning. In contrast, real estate moguls mitigate risk by diversifying property types and locations, leveraging strategic debt, and maintaining robust cash flow. The comparative analysis highlights the distinct approaches each sector takes to balance ambition with caution. The willingness to embrace calculated risks is a common thread that binds these entrepreneurial giants.

Silicon Valley's risk culture is rooted in the belief that failure is a stepping stone to success. Startups often iterate rapidly, learning from failures and pivoting to new strategies. This iterative approach allows them to adapt to changing market conditions and seize new opportunities. The availability of venture capital enables tech entrepreneurs to take bold risks without the fear of immediate financial ruin. This risk-taking culture is further supported by a network of mentors, advisors, and industry peers who provide guidance and support.

In the real estate sector, risk management is centered around diversification and strategic planning. Real estate moguls spread their investments across different property types and locations to minimize exposure to market fluctuations. They also leverage debt strategically, using it as a tool to amplify returns while maintaining a healthy cash flow. Real estate leaders conduct thorough due diligence, analyzing market trends, and economic indicators to make informed investment decisions. This disciplined approach to risk management allows them to navigate uncertainties and achieve consistent returns.

Both sectors employ strategies to mitigate risks and capitalize on rewards. In Silicon Valley, startups often pivot their business models based on market feedback and emerging trends. This agility allows them to stay ahead of competitors and capture new opportunities. Real estate moguls, on the other hand, rely on their deep market knowledge and strategic foresight to identify lucrative opportunities. They often engage in value-add projects, such as property renovations and repositioning, to enhance asset value and generate higher returns.

The comparative analysis of risk and reward highlights the unique strengths of each sector. Tech entrepreneurs thrive in an environment that rewards bold experimentation and rapid iteration. Their ability to adapt to changing conditions and pivot quickly is a key driver of success. Real estate moguls, meanwhile, excel in creating stable, long-term value through disciplined planning and diversification. Their strategic approach to risk management ensures consistent growth and resilience in the face of market volatility.

In summary, the contrasting approaches to risk and reward in Silicon Valley and the real estate industry reveal the diverse paths to entrepreneurial success. By understanding these differences, business leaders can gain valuable insights into how to balance ambition with caution and achieve sustainable growth in their respective fields.

4

Chapter 4: Culture and Leadership

Leadership styles in Silicon Valley and the real estate industry are shaped by their unique cultures. Tech visionaries foster environments that encourage experimentation, flat hierarchies, and open communication. Leaders like Elon Musk and Jeff Bezos are known for their bold visions and hands-on approaches. This chapter delves into the leadership strategies that drive innovation in the tech world, from fostering a culture of continuous learning to empowering teams to take calculated risks. Conversely, real estate leaders prioritize experience, relationships, and pragmatic decision-making. Their success relies on methodical planning and execution, underpinned by a stable and supportive corporate culture. The contrasting leadership philosophies offer insights into how each sector nurtures its talent and drives progress.

Silicon Valley's culture is characterized by a spirit of collaboration and innovation. Companies often adopt flat organizational structures that promote open communication and quick decision-making. This collaborative environment encourages employees to share ideas, experiment, and learn from failures. Leadership in Silicon Valley is often hands-on, with leaders actively involved in the day-to-day operations of their companies. They inspire their teams through visionary thinking, setting ambitious goals, and fostering a sense of purpose. This leadership style empowers employees to take ownership of their work and contribute to the company's success.

In the real estate sector, leadership is built on a foundation of experience and relationships. Real estate moguls have honed their skills through years of industry experience, developing a deep understanding of market dynamics and business operations. They build strong networks of relationships with stakeholders, from contractors and architects to government officials and investors. These relationships are essential for navigating the complexities of property development and ensuring successful project execution. Real estate leaders prioritize methodical planning and execution, ensuring that each project is completed on time and within budget.

The contrasting leadership styles in Silicon Valley and real estate highlight the importance of adaptability and strategic thinking. Tech leaders thrive in fast-paced environments that require quick decision-making and a willingness to experiment. Their ability to inspire and motivate teams is crucial for driving innovation and achieving ambitious goals. Real estate leaders, on the other hand, excel in driving stability and long-term value creation. Their strategic thinking and ability to build strong networks ensure the successful execution of complex projects.

The chapter also explores the importance of nurturing talent within each sector. Silicon Valley companies often implement programs that encourage continuous learning and professional development. Employees are given the freedom to explore new ideas and take risks, fostering a culture of innovation. Real estate leaders, on the other hand, invest in training and mentorship programs that develop the skills and knowledge of their teams. The focus is on building a workforce that can navigate the complexities of property development and management. Both sectors recognize the value of investing in their people as a key driver of success.

In summary, the leadership styles and cultures of Silicon Valley and the real estate industry are shaped by their unique environments and challenges. Tech visionaries thrive in a culture of innovation and experimentation, while real estate leaders excel in building stable, long-term value through experience and relationships. By understanding these leadership dynamics, we gain valuable insights into how each sector nurtures its talent and drives progress.

5

Chapter 5: Market Dynamics

Market dynamics play a crucial role in shaping the strategies of both Valley Vanguards and Realty Royals. The tech industry is characterized by rapid changes, where staying ahead of trends can make or break a company. This chapter explores how tech companies leverage data analytics, consumer insights, and agile methodologies to navigate market shifts. In real estate, market dynamics are influenced by factors such as economic cycles, interest rates, and demographic trends. Real estate moguls must anticipate these changes and adjust their strategies accordingly, whether it's through repositioning properties or expanding into new markets. The chapter provides a comparative look at how each sector responds to external forces and capitalizes on opportunities.

Silicon Valley companies operate in an environment of constant change and disruption. To stay competitive, they must continuously innovate and adapt to new technologies and market demands. Data analytics and consumer insights play a critical role in guiding strategic decisions. By analyzing market trends and consumer behavior, tech companies can identify emerging opportunities and tailor their products and services to meet evolving needs. Agile methodologies allow them to iterate quickly, bringing new solutions to market faster than traditional industries.

In the real estate sector, market dynamics are influenced by broader economic and demographic trends. Real estate leaders must stay attuned to changes in interest rates, housing demand, and population growth to make informed investment decisions. The ability to anticipate market shifts and adapt strategies accordingly is crucial for success. Real estate moguls often diversify their portfolios, investing in different property types and locations to mitigate risk. This strategic approach allows them to capitalize on opportunities and achieve consistent returns.

Both sectors employ strategies to navigate market dynamics and stay ahead of the competition. In Silicon Valley, companies often engage in partnerships and collaborations to access new technologies and markets. Strategic acquisitions and mergers are also common, allowing tech firms to expand their capabilities and market reach. Real estate leaders, on the other hand, focus on building strong relationships with stakeholders and leveraging their networks to identify and secure lucrative deals. The ability to build and maintain these relationships is a key factor in their success.

The comparative analysis of market dynamics reveals the unique strengths of each sector. Tech companies excel in their ability to innovate and adapt quickly to changing conditions. Their use of data analytics and agile methodologies allows them to stay ahead of trends and deliver solutions that meet consumer needs. Real estate moguls, meanwhile, excel in their ability to anticipate market shifts and make strategic investments that generate long-term value. Their deep market knowledge and strong networks provide a competitive advantage.

In summary, the strategies employed by Valley Vanguards and Realty Royals to navigate market dynamics highlight their unique strengths and approaches to business mastery. By understanding these differences, business leaders can gain valuable insights into how to capitalize on opportunities and achieve sustained growth in their respective fields.

6

Chapter 6: Funding and Capital

Securing funding is a critical aspect of business mastery. Silicon Valley startups often rely on venture capital, angel investors, and initial public offerings (IPOs) to fuel their growth. This chapter delves into the fundraising strategies employed by tech entrepreneurs, from pitching to investors to managing funding rounds. The availability of capital enables startups to experiment, iterate, and scale rapidly. Venture capital firms play a pivotal role in this ecosystem, providing not only financial backing but also strategic guidance and industry connections. The relationship between entrepreneurs and investors is symbiotic, with both parties working towards the common goal of achieving exponential growth.

Angel investors, often successful entrepreneurs themselves, provide early-stage funding and mentorship to fledgling startups. Their involvement goes beyond financial support; they offer valuable insights and advice based on their own experiences. This mentorship helps startups navigate the challenges of the early stages and lays the foundation for future success. Initial public offerings (IPOs) represent a significant milestone for tech companies, providing access to public capital markets and increasing visibility. The process of going public requires careful planning and execution, but the rewards can be substantial, including increased funding, market recognition, and the ability to attract top talent.

In contrast, real estate ventures typically rely on a combination of equity, debt, and private investments. Real estate moguls navigate the complexities of financing through leveraging assets, securing loans, and attracting institutional investors. Equity financing involves raising capital by selling shares in the property or project, while debt financing involves borrowing money to be repaid with interest. Real estate investment trusts (REITs) provide a way for investors to invest in real estate without directly owning properties, offering liquidity and diversification benefits. Private investments, such as joint ventures and partnerships, allow real estate leaders to pool resources and share risks.

The ability to structure financing deals effectively is a critical skill for real estate leaders. They must balance the need for capital with the goal of maximizing returns while minimizing risk. This involves carefully evaluating financing options, negotiating favorable terms, and managing relationships with investors and lenders. Real estate moguls often engage in creative financing strategies, such as using tax credits, grants, and incentives to reduce costs and enhance profitability. By leveraging their assets and expertise, they can secure the funding needed to bring ambitious projects to life.

In summary, the funding and capital strategies employed by Valley Vanguards and Realty Royals reveal the diverse paths to business mastery. Silicon Valley startups rely on venture capital, angel investors, and IPOs to fuel their rapid growth, while real estate ventures use a combination of equity, debt, and private investments to finance their projects. By understanding these differences, business leaders can gain valuable insights into how to secure the funding needed to achieve their visions and sustain growth.

7

Chapter 7: Technological Integration

While Silicon Valley is synonymous with technology, the real estate sector is increasingly integrating tech innovations to enhance efficiency and value. This chapter explores the intersection of technology and real estate, from smart buildings and property management systems to the rise of proptech startups. The adoption of technologies such as artificial intelligence, blockchain, and the Internet of Things (IoT) is transforming how properties are developed, managed, and marketed. The chapter highlights case studies of real estate companies that have successfully integrated technology to gain a competitive edge and improve the customer experience.

Smart buildings, equipped with advanced sensors and automation systems, optimize energy usage, enhance security, and improve occupant comfort. These intelligent structures use data analytics to monitor and control various building systems, such as heating, ventilation, air conditioning (HVAC), lighting, and security. By collecting and analyzing data in real-time, smart buildings can identify inefficiencies and implement corrective measures, reducing operating costs and environmental impact. Property management systems (PMS) streamline administrative tasks, such as lease management, maintenance requests, and tenant communications, improving operational efficiency and tenant satisfaction.

Blockchain technology is revolutionizing real estate transactions by providing a secure, transparent, and efficient way to record and transfer property ownership. Smart contracts, powered by blockchain, automate and enforce the terms of agreements, reducing the need for intermediaries and minimizing the risk of fraud. This technology enhances trust and transparency in real estate transactions, making the process faster and more efficient. Proptech startups are leveraging blockchain to create innovative solutions for property management, investment, and financing, driving the digital transformation of the real estate industry.

The Internet of Things (IoT) is another game-changer for the real estate sector. IoT devices, such as smart thermostats, security cameras, and occupancy sensors, collect data on various aspects of building operations and tenant behavior. This data provides valuable insights into how properties are used, enabling real estate leaders to make data-driven decisions that enhance efficiency and tenant satisfaction. For example, IoT-enabled predictive maintenance can identify potential issues before they become major problems, reducing downtime and maintenance costs. IoT also enables the creation of smart communities, where interconnected devices and systems enhance the quality of life for residents.

In summary, the integration of technology into the real estate sector is transforming how properties are developed, managed, and marketed. The adoption of smart buildings, property management systems, blockchain, and IoT is driving efficiency, transparency, and customer satisfaction. By embracing these innovations, real estate leaders can gain a competitive edge and create value for their stakeholders. The case studies of successful proptech startups highlight the potential of technology to reshape the real estate industry and pave the way for future growth.

8

Chapter 8: Customer-Centric Approaches

Understanding and meeting customer needs is a cornerstone of business success. Tech companies prioritize user experience, often employing user-centric design and iterative development processes. This chapter delves into how Silicon Valley firms gather and analyze user feedback to create products that resonate with their audience. User-centric design involves placing the needs and preferences of users at the forefront of the development process. By conducting user research, usability testing, and gathering feedback, tech companies can create intuitive and engaging products that meet the evolving needs of their customers. This iterative approach allows for continuous improvement and innovation.

Silicon Valley companies often employ agile methodologies, which prioritize flexibility, collaboration, and rapid iteration. Agile development involves breaking projects into smaller, manageable tasks, allowing teams to respond quickly to changes and incorporate user feedback throughout the process. This approach enables tech firms to deliver high-quality products that align with user expectations and market demands. The emphasis on user experience and customer satisfaction is a key driver of success for Silicon Valley companies, as it fosters loyalty and drives growth.

In the real estate sector, customer-centricity involves understanding tenant and buyer preferences, from location and amenities to sustainability features. Real estate leaders conduct market research and analyze demographic trends to identify the needs and preferences of their target audience. By offering properties that align with these preferences, real estate moguls can attract and retain tenants and buyers, increasing occupancy rates and property values. The focus on customer satisfaction extends to property management, where responsive service and proactive maintenance enhance the tenant experience.

Sustainability is an increasingly important factor for real estate customers. Tenants and buyers are seeking properties that offer energy efficiency, green building practices, and sustainable amenities. Real estate leaders are responding to this demand by incorporating sustainability features into their developments, such as solar panels, green roofs, and energy-efficient appliances. These features not only reduce environmental impact but also lower operating costs and enhance property value. By prioritizing sustainability, real estate moguls can attract environmentally conscious customers and create a positive brand image.

In summary, the customer-centric approaches of Silicon Valley and the real estate sector highlight the importance of understanding and meeting customer needs. Tech companies prioritize user experience and employ agile methodologies to create innovative products that resonate with their audience. Real estate leaders focus on tenant and buyer preferences, offering properties that align with their needs and incorporating sustainability features to enhance value. By adopting customer-centric strategies, businesses in both sectors can achieve success and drive growth.

Chapter 9: Innovation vs. Tradition

Innovation drives the tech industry, but the real estate sector is rooted in tradition. This chapter explores the tension between innovation and tradition in both industries. In Silicon Valley, companies that fail to innovate risk obsolescence, while in real estate, adhering to proven methods can be a safeguard against market volatility. The chapter examines how each sector balances the push for innovation with the need to maintain stability. Case studies of companies that have successfully navigated this balance provide insights into the strategies that can be employed to achieve sustained growth.

Silicon Valley thrives on innovation, with companies constantly pushing the boundaries of technology and challenging the status quo. The rapid pace of technological advancements creates an environment where staying ahead of the curve is essential for survival. Companies that fail to innovate risk becoming obsolete, as new competitors emerge with disruptive technologies. The emphasis on innovation drives continuous experimentation, iteration, and improvement, fostering a culture of creativity and risk-taking. However, this relentless pursuit of innovation can also lead to instability, as companies face the pressure to continuously deliver groundbreaking solutions.

In the real estate sector, tradition and stability are valued traits. Real estate moguls rely on proven methods and established practices to navigate the complexities of property development and management. The emphasis on tradition provides a sense of stability and predictability, which is essential for long-term success. Real estate leaders focus on meticulous planning, market analysis, and strategic execution to ensure the success of their projects. The reliance on tradition does not mean that innovation is absent; rather, it is carefully integrated into the established framework to enhance value and efficiency.

The tension between innovation and tradition is evident in both sectors. In Silicon Valley, companies must strike a balance between pushing the boundaries of technology and maintaining stability. This involves carefully managing resources, setting realistic goals, and ensuring that innovation efforts are aligned with long-term business objectives. Real estate leaders, on the other hand, must balance the need for stability with the desire to embrace new technologies and practices. This involves evaluating the potential benefits and risks of innovation and integrating new solutions in a way that complements traditional methods.

Case studies of companies that have successfully navigated this balance provide valuable insights. For example, tech firms that have achieved sustained growth often adopt a strategic approach to innovation, focusing on strategic goals and ensuring that their innovation efforts are sustainable. Similarly, real estate companies that successfully integrate innovation into their traditional frameworks often do so by adopting a phased approach, piloting new technologies and practices on a smaller scale before rolling them out more broadly.

The key takeaway from this chapter is the importance of finding the right balance between innovation and tradition. Both sectors can learn from each other's approaches, with tech companies adopting more disciplined planning and real estate leaders embracing new technologies. By striking this balance, businesses can achieve sustained growth, resilience, and long-term success.

9

Chapter 10: Global Expansion

Both Valley Vanguards and Realty Royals aspire to expand their influence globally. This chapter explores the challenges and opportunities associated with global expansion in each sector. Tech companies often expand rapidly, leveraging digital platforms to reach international markets. The chapter discusses the strategies employed by tech firms to adapt to different regulatory environments and cultural contexts. In contrast, real estate expansion involves navigating complex legal frameworks, building local partnerships, and understanding regional market dynamics. The chapter provides a comparative analysis of how each sector approaches global growth and the lessons that can be learned from their experiences.

Silicon Valley companies often adopt a digital-first approach to global expansion, leveraging the internet and digital platforms to reach customers worldwide. This allows them to scale rapidly and enter new markets with minimal physical presence. However, expanding internationally also presents challenges, such as navigating different regulatory environments, cultural differences, and local competition. Tech firms must adapt their products and services to meet the unique needs and preferences of each market. This involves conducting thorough market research, building local partnerships, and investing in localization efforts.

In the real estate sector, global expansion requires a more hands-on approach. Real estate leaders must navigate complex legal frameworks and build strong relationships with local stakeholders. This involves understanding local regulations, zoning laws, and market dynamics to identify opportunities and mitigate risks. Real estate moguls often partner with local developers, architects, and contractors to execute projects successfully. They must also consider cultural differences and preferences when designing and marketing properties. The ability to build and maintain these relationships is crucial for successful global expansion.

Both sectors face challenges and opportunities in their pursuit of global growth. Tech companies benefit from the scalability and reach of digital platforms, but they must navigate regulatory complexities and cultural nuances. Real estate leaders, on the other hand, must build local partnerships and navigate legal frameworks to succeed in new markets. The comparative analysis of global expansion strategies reveals the unique strengths and challenges of each sector and offers valuable insights for business leaders.

In summary, the global expansion strategies of Valley Vanguards and Realty Royals highlight the diverse approaches to achieving international growth. Tech companies leverage digital platforms to scale rapidly, while real estate leaders build local partnerships and navigate complex legal frameworks. By understanding these differences, business leaders can gain valuable insights into how to successfully expand their influence and achieve global growth.

10

Chapter 11: Sustainability and Ethics

Sustainability and ethical considerations are becoming increasingly important in both industries. Silicon Valley companies are under pressure to address environmental impacts and promote ethical practices in areas such as data privacy and labor conditions. This chapter explores how tech firms are incorporating sustainability into their business models, from reducing carbon footprints to fostering diversity and inclusion. In the real estate sector, sustainability involves creating energy-efficient buildings, promoting green construction practices, and contributing to community development. The chapter highlights case studies of companies that are leading the way in ethical and sustainable business practices.

Silicon Valley companies are increasingly recognizing the importance of sustainability and ethical practices. This involves reducing their environmental impact through initiatives such as energy-efficient data centers, renewable energy sourcing, and sustainable product design. Tech firms are also focusing on promoting diversity and inclusion within their organizations, creating inclusive workplaces that reflect the diverse communities they serve. Ethical considerations, such as data privacy and labor conditions, are also a priority, with companies implementing policies and practices to protect user data and ensure fair labor practices.

In the real estate sector, sustainability involves designing and constructing buildings that minimize environmental impact and promote energy efficiency.

Green building practices, such as using sustainable materials, incorporating renewable energy sources, and implementing water-saving technologies, are becoming standard in real estate development. Real estate leaders are also focusing on community development, creating spaces that enhance the quality of life for residents and contribute to the overall well-being of the community. This includes initiatives such as affordable housing, public spaces, and community services.

Both sectors are making strides in sustainability and ethics, driven by increasing awareness and demand from customers, investors, and regulators. The chapter highlights case studies of companies that are leading the way in these areas, showcasing innovative solutions and best practices. For example, tech firms that have successfully reduced their carbon footprints and promoted diversity and inclusion serve as role models for other companies. Similarly, real estate developers that have created energy-efficient buildings and contributed to community development demonstrate the potential for sustainable and ethical business practices.

In summary, the focus on sustainability and ethics is shaping the future of both Silicon Valley and the real estate sector. By incorporating sustainable and ethical practices into their business models, companies can create value for their stakeholders and contribute to a more sustainable and equitable world. The case studies highlighted in this chapter provide valuable insights and inspiration for business leaders looking to make a positive impact.

11

Chapter 12: Future Trends and Challenges

The final chapter looks ahead to the future trends and challenges that will shape the trajectories of Valley Vanguards and Realty Royals. The tech industry faces challenges such as regulatory scrutiny, cybersecurity threats, and the need for continuous innovation. Real estate companies must navigate evolving market conditions, changing demographics, and the impact of technological advancements. The chapter provides a forward-looking analysis of the key trends that will influence each sector, from the rise of artificial intelligence and blockchain to the increasing importance of sustainable development. By understanding these trends, business leaders can better prepare for the future and continue to achieve mastery in their respective fields.

One of the key trends shaping the tech industry is the rise of artificial intelligence (AI) and machine learning. These technologies have the potential to revolutionize various aspects of business, from automating processes and enhancing decision-making to creating new products and services. Companies that successfully integrate AI into their operations can gain a competitive edge and drive innovation. However, the widespread adoption of AI also presents challenges, such as ethical considerations, data privacy, and the potential for job displacement.

In the real estate sector, technological advancements are transforming how properties are developed, managed, and marketed. The adoption of smart building technologies, blockchain, and the Internet of Things (IoT) is enhancing efficiency, transparency, and tenant satisfaction. Real estate leaders must stay attuned to these trends and invest in the technologies that will drive future growth. Additionally, changing demographics, such as the aging population and the rise of remote work, are influencing demand for different types of properties. Real estate companies must adapt their strategies to meet these evolving needs.

Sustainability will continue to be a key focus for both sectors. As awareness of environmental issues grows, companies must prioritize sustainable practices to meet customer and regulatory demands. This includes reducing carbon footprints, promoting energy efficiency, and creating sustainable products and properties. Companies that lead the way in sustainability can enhance their brand reputation and create long-term value for their stakeholders.

The chapter also highlights the importance of resilience and adaptability in the face of future challenges. Both Valley Vanguards and Realty Royals must navigate regulatory scrutiny, economic uncertainties, and geopolitical risks. By building resilient business models and fostering a culture of innovation and adaptability, companies can better prepare for the future and achieve sustained growth.

In summary, the future trends and challenges facing Silicon Valley and the real estate sector highlight the need for continuous innovation, technological integration, and sustainable practices. By understanding these trends and preparing for future challenges, business leaders can continue to achieve mastery in their respective fields and create value for their stakeholders. The insights and strategies shared in this chapter provide a roadmap for navigating the dynamic and ever-evolving business landscape.

Book Description:

"Valley Vanguards and Realty Royals: Comparative Business Mastery" delves into the contrasting worlds of Silicon Valley's tech titans and the steadfast real estate moguls, offering an in-depth analysis of their unique approaches to business success. Across twelve comprehensive chapters, the book explores the core principles, strategies, and leadership styles that define

CHAPTER 12: FUTURE TRENDS AND CHALLENGES

these two sectors.

Key Features:

1. **Innovation vs. Stability:** Discover how Silicon Valley thrives on disruptive innovation while real estate empires are built on stable, long-term value creation.
2. **Risk and Reward:** Compare the high-stakes environment of tech startups with the calculated risk management of real estate investments.
3. **Leadership Dynamics:** Learn about the visionary leadership that drives tech giants and the experienced, relationship-based leadership in the real estate sector.
4. **Market Adaptation:** Understand how each sector navigates market dynamics, leveraging data analytics in tech and strategic planning in real estate.
5. **Global Expansion and Sustainability:** Examine the strategies for global growth and the increasing importance of ethical and sustainable practices in both industries.

Filled with insightful comparisons, real-world case studies, and practical lessons, "Valley Vanguards and Realty Royals" provides a compelling guide for business leaders and entrepreneurs looking to master their respective fields and achieve sustained growth.

www.ingramcontent.com/pod-product-compliance
Lightning Source LLC
LaVergne TN
LVHW020744090526
838202LV00057BA/6227